Concert and Contest COLLECTION

Compiled and Edited by H. VOXMAN

for

Bb BASS CLARINET with piano accompaniment

CONTENTS

RUBANK®

HAL•LEONARD® CORPORATION
7777 W. BLUEMOUND RD. P.O. BOX 13819 MILWAUKEE, WI 53213

Sarabande and Bourrée
from First French Suite

Bb Bass Clarinet

J. S. BACH
Transcribed by R. Hervig

Patrol Russe

Bb Bass Clarinet

V. VOLOSCHINOV
Transcribed by H. Voxman

Mosaic

Bb Bass Clarinet

R. H. WALTHEW
Transcribed by H. Voxman

Largo and Allegro Vivace
from Sonata in B♭ Major

Bb Bass Clarinet

J. B. LOEILLET
Transcribed by H. Voxman

Two Russian Pieces

Bb Bass Clarinet

V. KALINIKOFF
Transcribed by H. Voxman

I – LAMENT

* Add top side key to play B.

Bb Bass Clarinet

II - SCHERZO

V. KOSSENKO
Transcribed by H. Voxman

* Use chromatic fingering for B.

Concerto No. 8 in Bb

Bb Bass Clarinet

G. F. HANDEL
Transcribed by H. Voxman

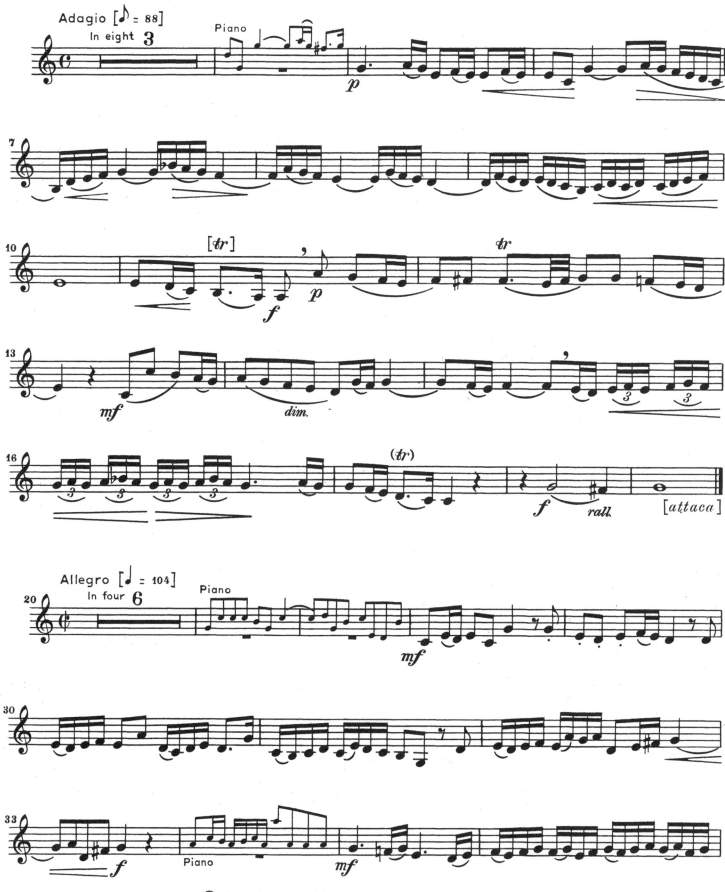

Largo and Allegro
from Sonata I, Op. 3

B♭ Bass Clarinet

Realization by
R. Hervig

J. B. LOEILLET
Transcribed by H. Voxman

Romance and Troika
from Lieutenant Kijé Suite

Bb Bass Clarinet

SERGE PROKOFIEFF
Arr. by Herman A. Hummel

Divertissement in B♭

Bb Bass Clarinet

F. J. HAYDN
Transcribed by R. Hervig

Concertino in D Minor

Bb Bass Clarinet

LEROY OSTRANSKY

Sonatina

B♭ Bass Clarinet

RICHARD HERVIG

Chincoteague

Bb Bass Clarinet

CLARENCE E. HURRELL

Scherzando (♩ = 96)

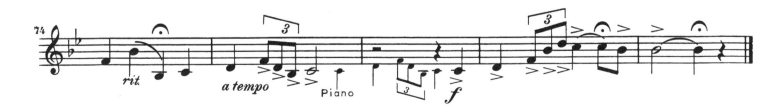

Andante
from Concerto in Bb Major

Bb Bass Clarinet

A. BEON
Transcribed by H. Voxman

Minuet and Gigue
from Suite No. 1 for Solo Cello

Bb Bass Clarinet
(Unaccompanied)

J. S. BACH
Transcribed by H. Voxman

Minuet (♩ = 104)

Gigue (♩. = 108)